Words for Becoming

Anna Jollymore

EMPRESS
PUBLICATIONS
WWW.EMPRESSPUBLICATIONS.COM

I dedicate this book to my mother, my grandmothers,
and all my great-grandmothers before me,
who never stopped searching for mercy.

Table of Contents

Introduction

There comes a moment in every transformation
when you're no longer who you were –
but not yet who you are becoming.
This book was born in that in-between.

Words for Becoming is a collection of transmissions
from my own Hero's Journey.
They came through while I was breaking old myths,
surviving initiations,
learning how to let the sacred be messy,
and how to hold the mess sacred.

Some of these words will soothe you.
Others may provoke.

Read them like spells.
Read them like stories.
Read them like echoes and chimes and thunderclaps.

And above all,
let them help you *re-member:*

You are not too much.
You are not too late.
You are already in it.
Your becoming is well underway.

Welcome

The magic of this container gently murmurs in the stillness with a buzzing genderless voice:

Wake up.

It is safe now to receive.

Oh, Pluto

Wrestling with the existential dread
of how much I am shifting and changing.

The moment of hot choking steam and confusion –

Right before one wipes the fog from the mirror.

Whose eyes will I meet in my vanity this morning?

A twig snaps.
A bird caws.

And somewhere in the mists of a dark and distant forest
high up in the trees –

I can hear the sound of my Wild Twin climbing,
singing,
laughing –

Free.

Incendiary Devices

I dreamt this morning that I read aloud a poem
Filled with such stark and naked truths
That the headlines in the paper later read:

LOCAL WRITER ARRESTED FOR INDECENT EXPOSURE

What words can I strike together like flint?
What dangerous portals can I open?
What can I say to burn down your house,

Leaving nothing but a smoking crater behind
That someday might be reclaimed by nature
All vines and mud and twitching, singing insects
Turning their faces up to the rain?

Not Four but Six Agreements

(Inspired by *The Four Agreements*
by Don Miguel Ruiz)

I am impeccable in thought, word, and deed.
I make no assumptions.
I take nothing personally.
I try my best.
I intuitively follow the Laws of Nature.
I serve the world through Magic Words,
with the goal of healing the heart of the empire.

I am, That I am,
and so it is,
with love and gratitude
for all that is to come.

You Can Ask for a Different Kind of Teacher

Woke up today thinking about Pain as my teacher,
And the phrase "You can ask for a different kind of teacher"
On my mind.

If that's true, then I call down Surrender as my next teacher
And welcome in lessons of ease and softness.

I release my need to control everything,
And my hypervigilance,
To the extent that I'm currently able,
In order to make space for these new experiences.

I am ready to fall in love with everything and everyone,
With life itself,
Exactly as it is.

Where the River Meets the Sea

I had a great fear that I was a mile wide
But only an inch thick,

And so I dove and strove for depth
And in the great tradition of all try-hards before me –

Dug myself a trench,
Which became my grave.

I stopped trying and started praying,
As one does in trenches, at graves,

And to my surprise – I became a river,
Traveling home to meet the sea.

Navigating

Moving from healing to Healer involves
a significant shift in perspective,
no longer healing as a freedom from pain and suffering
but healing as a transformation, integration, and ascension.

Healing as a "front-facing" motion,
a move toward what IS wanted.
Not a move away from what is UNwanted.
(That's called coping – useful, but not the same.)

It's the difference between running out of a collapsing
building, and navigating a ship through the stars.

Where Do the Women in My Family Put Their Pain?

Where do the women in my family put their pain?
It is not stored in our cellars, like
apples or onions or jam.

My mother wears it around her waist like a great innertube.
She lumbers and settles heavily into chairs,
and with bitterness broadcasts plainly that
the weight of all her unrequited longings will quite literally
be the death of her,
and the forever embrace of the too-tight coffin is too little,
too late.
Instead, she requests this dignity –
to be incinerated so as to know glowing heat at least once, to be
scattered in the wind and know lightness at long last.
Finally free of all her fears and regrets,
the cold indifference of an unforgiving world,
and her three ungrateful children.

My grandmothers put their pain into their hands;
it flowed down their arms like sticky ochre poison.
It landed hard across cheeks,
so that the small piercing cries of shame and helpless surprise
could be heard externally as a brief exorcism.
Ragged wisps of ghosts that didn't go too far –
not with stinging handprints to keep the generational curse

pressed in close,
like the nettles that grow around fence posts in Iowa.

My sister focused not on the ghost but on the exorcism itself,
excising parts of her self bit by bit,
labeling them in hermetically sealed jars
or pinned beneath glass in memoriam.
She has removed so much by her late thirties
that the rest is now organically sloughing off in dry coils here,
in heavy piles of rot there.
Only in her face, her eyes, does she keep a small piece of
identity that sighs
with the relief of a mother who has managed to shield her children
from the waves and waves of radiation that roll atomically across
the wasteland of our family.
She shields her children with her own body, from her own body.
Fragmented, fading, receding ever deeper
into her own shell of a body,
the light in her eyes passing more and more
to her children each year
who will know her love by name,
but never her sacrifice, and that is by design.
Her pain is her privacy, her deliberation, her strength.
Her demise alone.

And mine?

I've scattered my pain like wildflower seeds into ditches.
I've smuggled it across state lines.
I've passed it on to lovers, and more than one friend.
I've used it to burn my candle at both ends.

I've resolved to defeat it!
I've dissolved, I've surrendered.
And now in my 40th year –
I seek to turn my body
into the cup that can hold it gracefully while it is still potable.
Before the wine turns to vinegar.

That I might drink it and piss it away,
back to Earth Mother as water and salt
and other assorted minerals.

Somewhere in time, the women in my family forgot how to give
their pain back to Earth Mother,
the only mother with a body big enough to transmute it all
without cannibalizing self or other.

I crane my head back and open my mouth up to the rain.
I try my very best to re-member.

The Push and The Pull

Had a real moment last night –
seeing the "Pull Forces" of certain energies,
realizing I'm experiencing them as "Push Forces"
when really it's the other way around.

No wonder there are so many messages about surrendering,
Becoming Empty, Trusting the Universe.

You don't have to try so hard.

All that matters is releasing resistance.

Where We Get Into Trouble

Feelings are always real and valid,
And absolutely hugely important.
People pretend feelings can't be measured or proven
But feelings are sensations that literally happen in the body.
There is plenty of evidence for the materialists.

Meaning, however, is highly contextual,
And this is where we get into trouble.
Because we want to turn feelings into stories,
And then turn those stories into The Truth.

Remember that feelings are sensations in the body.
And while they are always real and valid,
They aren't unilaterally *true*.

Feelings are the questions, not the answers.

Working With My Parts

Exploring the feeling of Vulnerability today –
Like a throbbing in my chest.

An openness.

I feel exposed.
I am working with my parts who are scared and screaming,
Trying to assure them that it's all okay
And that I will protect them from violence.
Because I believe this feeling is good!

It is the feeling of an open heart,
And the start of exhilarating experiences.

I Eat Sin

People are afraid of responsibility
Because they're afraid they'll wield it poorly
Especially when it comes to making decisions
That could result in causing harm.

So they hire me, The Sin Eater, to take over their responsibility –
To take action,
Make the decisions,
Be the Messenger,
Make a meal out of it
And metabolize all the karma that comes with it.

This got twisted over time,
Through the increasingly narcissistic bend
Of our collective lens...
People worry less and less these days about harming others,
More and more about getting hurt themselves.

Still, people want to be insulated from consequence.
That hasn't changed.
Decisions are still the throughline, the interesting part.

I love making decisions.
Decisions are the mini deaths and births of
What comes (and goes!) immediately next,
In ways that change the course of the long term too.

The Ethical Trickster

Big twilight realization, loud as thunder –

You are not a trustworthy person.

This is a hard fault to look at, but I can't deny it's true.
It always will be, in a way, because I am a Trickster.

But the thing is, scorpions need love too...

So, how will I continue to build love and connection,
Now that this information's good and stuck in my craw?

It feels like a barrier to intimacy for sure,
And yet,
I feel optimism breaking through...
Because I am accepting of myself more,
I am more of my whole self when I let this information in,
And that is more important to intimacy than being perfect.
To bring my whole self, claws and all,
into relationship is the entire point!
I just need to figure out how to do it respectfully,
Artfully and transparently.
In ways that do no harm to the people I care about.

Perhaps I could even pen *The Ethical Trickster:*
A Guide to Love and Friendship with the God of Mischief.

But then again, who would ever read it and believe it?

Grief

Powerless – one of the most excruciating
And thrilling emotions to stay present in.

We tend to not attune to where we feel the most powerless.
And grief is one of those things,
Where we tend to feel the most powerless.
And so a great many people are willfully blind to it.

Strengthen your skills for withstanding that discomfort,
Build yourself a grief tool kit, and look –
And you will begin to see vast worlds shake and shimmer into Being
That have, in fact, been there all along.

Low Self-Esteem

Low Self-Esteem:
A state of total amnesia where one has forgotten what it feels like to have what is internally valued match what is externally valued.

Running Toward, Running Away

Running toward something is a very similar frequency
to running away from something,
and quite easily mistaken for it.

The wise don't run.
They cultivate stillness and draw their dreams to them
through miracles, synchronicities, and other delights.

They become magnets to their own authentic desires,
through the long work of worthiness and alignment.

They become holy wells in and of themselves...
Places that others pilgrimage to, bringing gifts,
in hopes of experiencing the vibration of miracles.

And how will they find you if you're always on the run?
Learn how to be Here, Now.
This is the secret place of maximum leverage.

The Oracle & The Magician:
A Poem to Summon Robert

I will pick up this pen and write my lover into my arms
(as if by magic):

In the middle of nowhere he came across
A woman who could not lie to him.

She spoke only in diamonds,
Clear and bright,
Utterly transparent.

She warned him that with great power comes great responsibility
She showed him all her boundaries
She told him that if he ever transgressed them
She would be gone by the morning.
She trusted him to ask respectful questions
And he trusted himself, because he trusted her.

To witness her bloom sincerely
Under the warmth of his gaze and adoration,
This woman with the indigo throat and diamond speech,
Caused his own heart to melt each and every time.

And so she stood armorless in the face of his love,

And he in hers,
Both bathed in pure radiance.

And they were perfect harmony,
Ecstatic in human form.

And so it is.

Shadow Child

Pre-birth, I rejected my entire Self
and I have been ashamed of my own existence ever since.

A Shadow Child, they said,
born without innocence.

With great glowing discs for eyes
to better peer into the dark.

The Last Days of Your 30s

Today is the last day of your thirties!

How will you savor it?
How will you remember it?

I will appreciate my body.
I will rejoice in the comfort and abundance of my home.
I will feel my feet on the ground and the sun on my face.
I will clear my head to make space for more goodness.
I will keep the energy of my space clean and flowing.
I will tell the people I love that I care about them.
I will notice all the ways my life is blessed and give thanks.

Today is my victory lap.

The Soft Path

The Soft Path isn't actually finding the path that contains the fewest harsh obstacles, although it is the very definition of the Path of Least Resistance!

It is an internal calibration, a surrender and acceptance, fully, of whatever comes next with a focused intention for the Highest Good of the Collective. The Soft Path *becomes* the path of least resistance when we release our resistance to it, therefore obstacles are no longer obstacles, whether "real" or "imagined."

All is recognized as a way of belonging.

All is perceived as the Elixir of Life – Adventure! – and all is welcomed with wonder.
Life becomes the sweet game of Mystery Unfolding,
playing each hand we are dealt.

I believe this is what Jim Henson was trying to teach us
with rhyme, rubber chickens, and felt.

A Second Moon

Welcome, Goddess.
Welcome Home!
Welcome home to your body.
Welcome home to the seat of our hearts, your Center.
Thank you for the wisdom you bring,
For the beauty and grace and harmony
you restore all along your path.
Welcome, Maiden, eyes bright with wonder and possibility!
Welcome Mother, full and wanting more.
Welcome Wise Woman of the Woods,
thank you for your medicine.
Welcome, Crone, the return of The Elder.
Our hearts have been made ready for this day,
for this time,
for the dawn of this age.
We use our freedom to birth the new dawn...
We choose to witness Her Rise.

Samhain 2024

One Father,
Two Husbands,
Three Mothers,

Let the next leg of the Spiral begin!
I welcome death and rebirth.
I hold my highest good firmly in my grasp.
I know I am not alone this time.
And I know where I am going –
Divinity.
X

What Is

*What would it mean for me, the world, the people I love, reality
itself, if this is the defining contrast of my perspective –
that all people, places, and things are exactly 50% amazing and 50% tragic,
that those two experiences are always existing side by side and neither
detracts from the other, they only serve to highlight and enhance one
another, that wherever I cast my gaze the light of my awareness exposes
more shadow, therefore there will always be more shadow exposed, more
awareness of fracture waiting to be incorporated back into wholeness and
thus creating fundamental changes to my perception of both What Is as
the sum of that newly formed wholeness and the scope of What Is
Unknown just beyond it, and this is why change is the only real constant...*

*This is why grounding and embodiment and presence are the keys to the
kingdom, to heaven on earth, because as the aperture continues to widen,
widen, widen the best place to find solace is the noticing of this exact
moment right here, right now, and the noticing that in this particular
moment all is peace, all is comfort, all is connection, all is well.*

99% of life can be the noticing of these moments.

Love Your Own Brand

I once knew a guy who insisted
That he liked to fart under the covers
And then cocoon inside of his bedsheets
Like a beautiful, blissed out little stink moth.

He absolutely insisted, and I quote:

"You've gotta love your own brand."

Brigid and Susan and Venus and Oya

Well he's slinked out of the house now
Off to hide from me and lick his wounds
After seven hours in the car
To Susan's father's funeral and back.

Where I told him I was frustrated
And he hollered in my face
That he could not, would not, would never never ever
Be able to empathize with my need for silence
And thus we slept in different beds,
In a cold and helpless rift.

Oh well.

Yesterday was Imbolc,
And although I did not do my ritual as planned
I did successfully collect thirty-three blessings
from my Community!
One for each vertebra.
And today my spine is on fire.
I think Brigid is at work yet.
I saw a chalk drawing of her in the vestibule of Baker Street.
Just like Venus, she was sleeping peacefully
Under a crescent moon.

Today is the feast day of Oya (or St. Teresa if you prefer) –
I will take my body, fire and all, to that celebration,
While trying to come to terms with this experience –

That I called my husband a coward, out loud, to his face.
(And while I do not believe that's true, in aggregate)
In that moment,
I really, really meant it.

Forest of Many Trees

Each love is a forest of many trees.
Stay under the canopy of just one tree for too long
And you may find it loses its magic.

Best to roam,
Slowly but surely,
Seeking new foliage to admire and
New scruff of bark under hand
Across the acres of canopy.

Do let your hands guide the way –
The body translates what the trees communicate.

Seeds

Maybe some "dead" things are simply inert.
Like a seed.

Not alive yet, but carrying the potential to be.
Just waiting for the right conditions.

I can take the buried stone from my heart and plant it here like the
pit of a fruit –
Restoring land, restoring myself, restoring sustenance.

Or maybe my heart is a walnut?
Or an acorn.

Projections

In order to truly embrace multidimensional awareness
One must truly embrace the existential horror
That "consensus reality" doesn't actually exist.
Or if it does –
It's just a teensy weensy
Tiny sliver
Of what we assume it to be.

And the world is RADICALLY different
In terms of moment-to-moment perception and experience
For each and every person.

And the vast majority of what we think we're observing
What we think we see
What we think we know
About everyone, about anyone –

Their personality, their behaviors,
Their vices, their virtues,
Their values, their hopes, their dreams and expectations,
Their desires, their preferences,
Their outlook on the world –
Are actually just projections of ourselves that we've cast upon
All the parts of them we can't see or don't understand.

Every person contains oceans of inner self,
Only 5% explored by any surface-dweller,
A stat that often includes the very self in question.

Don't believe me?
Ask an introvert.

You've got to really soak this in:

There are as many "truths" as there are points of perspective.
Hence, the multiverse manifesting within the same timeline
And proliferating with infinite complexity across all.

There is no Truth.
There never was and there never will be.
There are only Laws of Nature.

What Does it Take to
Forgive a Father?

I had a dream that my father died.

I was standing under an endless sky at sunset.
The porch was crumbling.
It smelled like field dirt and diesel, gravel and hay.
The old farm.

My mother and sister were there.
The navy blue twilight was overtaking the colors in the clouds.
We were admiring the quilt on his bed.
It was made by his friend – a woman named Ann Margaret.
"Did you know her?" I asked my sister.
"Not really, I had the privilege of meeting her a few times," she
replied.

How strangely vivid, all this imagery.
These aren't memories.
I don't know any Ann Margaret.

I feel paralyzed with fear now,
that any part of this dream might be prophetic.

And I feel at a loss,
that I still have any feeling at all of "home"
still rooted in the old farm.

Certainly in the Great Plains.
In the endless sky.
Sky as Ocean,
Horizon as the very curve of the Earth.

But why can't I separate the sky from him?
And his crooked hands, bent with arthritis,
holding a navy blue handkerchief.
And the way he always puts one hand on his hip
when he goes to blow his nose,
just the same as Gram'ma used to
with her own bent arthritic hands.

Mantras for the Fully Ensouled

I Am.
I Feel.
I Want.
I Do.
I Love.
I Speak.
I See.
I Know.
I Become.
I Accept.
I Forgive.
I Create.
I Will.

Crushed

The hours.
THE HOURS I could spend day-dreaming, let me tell you.

Reading into every conversation, every glance.
Replaying the sound of his laughter over and over in my head.
Making mental collages of all my favorite parts of him – the subtle
cleft in his chin, the copper flecks in his eyes, the deep timbre of his
voice rumbling in his perfect throat, the way his thin cotton t-shirts
clung to the curved musculature of his back, chest, and arms, and of
course – his thick, sinuous wrists.

It was shameful, what I was doing, and I'm not the kinda gal
who blushes easily.

But this was truly, voyeuristically shameful.
And the shame just made it hotter.

It was a thrilling time, if I'm being perfectly honest.
It felt so specifically intimate,
so wolfish and hexed
to jerk off to a real live person,
not just some character in a book or film.

A person I had been near enough that day to graze shoulders
with. Whose scent I could still conjure.

The hopelessly unproductive weeks I could spend lying supine under
the ceiling fan of my bedroom, an array of toys laid out on the towel
next to me, just thinking about those fingers.
Those hands.
Those wrists.

I know I'm not alone in this –

A good wrist is everything.

As a deeply interior person (and a Scorpio, if that isn't obvious by
now) I have always languished in the pleasure of a secret crush.

The unspeakable kind,
the crush NO ONE can know about
because it would be too dangerous to unleash upon the world,
its contents far too taboo.
Too impossible.
Too *forbidden*.

The kind of crush that lives and dies its entire life cycle
inside of my own head,
groaning against the ethereal constraints of imagination,
aching from the tangible absence of touch,
but in all other ways unbound
and free to live out a thousand lives,

a thousand delicious scenarios
at the behest of no one else's permission or approval.

For instance – the high school crush on a close long-time friend
that could never be more, and the vivid memories I have of an
imagined first kiss pressed against the side of a dusty old pick-up
truck on a dark gravel road...
Until a trilling bell condensed me back into the reality that I was in
fact sitting in Econ class, surrounded by the din of chittering
classmates snapping their books closed,
rustling papers and chairs scraping back
as they migrated on to the next period
and I came back into my body with a level of whiplash
I assume only time travelers can relate to.

Or the work crush on a married boss twenty years my senior, and all
the times I had to avoid making direct eye contact
or else risk losing my train of thought mid-presentation in a meeting
surrounded by coworkers. The number of MBTA seats left
dampened with the only evidence of my musings,
that someday we just might happen to bump into each other
outside of work,
decide to share a few cocktails,
maybe catch some live music together on a whim
at one of those dank and dark underground venues of Boston where
the drinks are stiff and the quarters are close enough that our bodies
might innocently nudge against one another,
setting off a cascade of chemical reactions that would demand
satisfaction despite our better judgement...

I can't tell you very many state capitals
or how to do long division
or what my old phone number was from the house I grew up in. I've
lost a hundred faces and twice that in names over the years.
But these crushes are the kind of memories I hold onto,
all the more precious because they are pristinely mine alone and
they remain perfect to this day inside a bubble
that has never been pierced by the cold disappointment of reality.

There should be a word (besides delusion) for the phenomena of
fantasies that live just as powerfully in the body,
and carry the same emotional resonance,
as any flesh-and-blood event.

Prima Materia

Last night, dreamily wondering about the Priestesses
and how they come again at death (the fullest, final kind)
and how they weep holy tears, cleansing tears,
that form the River Styx.

Our fathers leave us coins to pay the Ferryman,
but the river to the Underworld is feminine energy.

Prima Materia.

The waters that flow between worlds,
fed by tears and accompanied by wailing –
whether in death or in birth –
as in Her other form, the Waters of Life.

Enough salt water to fill all the oceans.
As deep as Hell.

And think of all the layers of sediment this water must traverse back
up through to emerge as nourishment from a human breast?

A Curse for the Modern Slumlords of Chicago

The first one will flee when the winter pipes burst.
The second will exit this space in a hearse.
The third one will squat for a year without rent.
The fourth will be cuffed after exploding meth.
Five will bring five hairy beasts who will spray
Every inch of the floor 'til the hardwood decays.
Six will bring chaos and juvenile delinquents,
Who will fan six more neighbors into flames most litigious.
Seven will mourn a new floor mucked and flooded.
Eight will see fridge, stove, and dishwasher gutted.
And finally, the ninth will look up in sheer wonder
To see blue sky revealed when the roof falls asunder.

Fifty-eight thousand three hundred and twenty.
Threefold the profit you wanted to bleed me.
Ruin and wreck, just rewards for your greed.
Ninefold your curses, and so mote it be.

What Is Real?

Q: What is real?
A: What you choose.

So What If I Am Plato?

So what if I am Plato or Socrates?

I am one of the Aphorists – crafting densely packed thought forms
to wake people and shake people
and shape reality to my will.

Just as Plato used philosophy (sculpting and activating with words)
to create an entire society for the Western World (and if that's not a
metaphor for a consensus reality, I don't know what is).

Well then, I can certainly create my own personal philosophy
to define my own personal reality!
And in doing so, shift the lens for my entire fractal...
Which in turn will ripple out
and influence other consensus realities,
because this, this is power, and power influences innately!

And here's the best part of all –

Like the mad shaman at the edge of the woods,
the significance of whose works is discovered later
by brighter, younger minds better able to place them in action –

I can do all this quietly and mostly in private,
whilst dithering around my home in peaceful obscurity,
bothering no one, and with no one's permission,
simply finding myself a hoot and a half.

A God with No Hands

Is this why I keep having visions of a god with no hands?

Philosophers don't build the future with their own hands...
But they do design the blueprints for it!

Is that one of my powers?
Is that THE power that's been (t)here all along?
If I design them, that means I can change them.
I can change the blueprints.
Through my own day-to-day experience...
How I live my life, the central point of my origin
(my value set, my paradigm),
The decisions I make,
My desires, my actions,
The energy I bring into the world.

The only immutable piece is my core essence.

A god with no hands, but a god nonetheless.

The Bargain

Belonging and Sorrow, what an interesting continuum.
Is this why The Hanged One was hung?
Because they spoke truth to power?
Is that the bargain we make as Tricksters?
Ultimate Knowledge
Ultimate Power
Ultimate Sacrifice
Ultimate Price
These all share the same home address.
Are you certain you still want to live there?
Now that you know that authenticity
requires dying a thousand deaths a day?
Twirling and dangling upside down from the world tree?
Plucking an eye out to place in Mimir's well?
Yes.
Yes I do.
Signed in ink.
Signed in blood.
Watch it sink
down into the cauldron –
And * tic * tic * tic * whoosh *
goes the pilot light catching.

Lost & Found

The way to not feel lost and fearful in the sea
Is to become the whole sea.
So too, with humanity.

I Wish

The thing about wishes, is that they are clues to desires.
And these clues are not to be underestimated.

When you whisper "I wish..."
What you're saying is "I want... I just don't believe I can have."

So understand your desires,
Pay attention to those whispers.

Follow them, trace them back to the roots –

The longing.
The hunger.
The unmet need.

Then ask, "What limiting belief created this woeful state of lack?"

Where is my shoe stuck in the mud?

And dare I liberate myself and run feral,

Half-barefoot and screaming into the night?

They say Helen's face launched a thousand ships.

Of course.

Wars are devised for greed, but fought for beauty.

No one takes up banners,
No one risks life and limb
For anything less than love.

And oh, how we wish for love –

That longing.
That hunger.
That unmet need.

All cowering and crouching beneath the weight of Belief.

Abused. Exhausted. Neglected. Negated.
Starving to death as the void ever widens.
"I wish..." for the courage to resurrect love.

Meet thy Desires, Meet Thyself.
Embrace thy Desires, Embrace Thyself.

Move thy Desires, Move Thyself.
Satisfy thy Desires, Satisfy Thyself.

It is not enough to Know alone.
Love demands an experience.

Don't let that Trickster Spirit, Belief,
Have you go thinking otherwise.

The Birthing Sight

In this time,
We must develop a Birthing Sight,
Birthing Vision,
Birthing Eyes.

And we must take up the call to action
And joyfully serve in this birthing process
According to the unique capabilities
Of each, as feels most natural.

Initiation

It happened at a Christmas party.

Chicago. Logan Square.

Many years ago.

There's a particular style of apartment in Logan Square – boxy three-story numbers. Old, with chipping beige paint and a lot of beautiful wood trim in various states of decay. Spiral staircases up the front and back, wood creaking under your feet as you pass landings cluttered with the neighbors' coats and boots and umbrellas and you can hear the music thumping from the top floor as you wind up, up and around, out of the cold and into a dark room congested with humans and radiator heat.

Have you ever looked at someone, and right away, right down to your very core, you just KNEW?

If you have, then you know exactly what I'm talking about.

If you haven't, then the Fates have spared you.
Or forsaken you.

I suppose it depends on your perspective on the whole thing.

But for me, looking at him, I JUST. FUCKING. KNEW.

I knew beyond the shadow of a doubt that somewhere, somehow.
Something was going to happen between us.

He was sitting in the dark on a piano bench when I first saw
him, under a pastel glow of worn-out old Christmas lights, amidst
the din of the party and the beige paint
and the decaying wood trim and the heavy sweaters
and the discordant overlapping sounds of laughter
and the plastic cups of cheap wine and whiskey
being passed all around.

The very second I laid eyes on him, my heart skipped a beat. And I
do not mean metaphorically, I mean it literally stopped for a full
second in a way that dumped adrenaline straight into my
bloodstream like I had just encountered a lion on the Serengeti.

It was intensely physical,
instant gravity.
The closest thing I can compare it to is vertigo –
that woozy feeling of tipping upside down,
ass over elbow,
into the abyss.

And the phrase I thought to myself in that tumbling instant –
as clear as a banner, urgent as a siren,
and ominous as church bells tolling – was *Uh oh.*

I have a theory now that 'love at first sight' is actually the
phenomena of encountering someone that you will have such
an intense connection with in the future
that it reverberates all the way back to the present.
The initiatory moment.

The resonance of that vibration imparts the world-tilting
knowledge:
"Here it is, the thing that's going to change everything..."
but then provides no other useful information
as it passes on through you like an apparition.

It's very disorienting.

Because how could someone I've never met nor know anything
about evoke such an immediate feeling, such a profound response?
This random guy in the plain burgundy wool sweater and the camel-
colored corduroys going threadbare around the knees? This –
perfect – stranger with the jutting chin, hawk nose, and chipped
front tooth... I mean... THIS guy???

It doesn't make any sense!!

I don't know what to say.

There was just something about him.

I was done for in a moment's glance.

It wasn't a cognitive function, it was an evolution.

A spontaneous adaptation that my body made
to accommodate the shape of him into my new reality.
The weight of it still lingers within me,
still pulling my guts floorward like it just happened yesterday.

My eyes did not leave him for the rest of that night.
I watched him talk to the others, and savored the deep sound
of his voice and the slight West Coast lilt to his speech pattern.
I watched his hazel-green eyes crinkle when he laughed.
I watched his thighs fidget and clench atop the altar of that sacred
piano bench, I watched his calloused hands wrap around his plastic
cup, and the nervous flick of his tongue sweeping over that chipped
front tooth amidst and between all of the chit chat.

I didn't dare talk to him though. No.
Not yet.
Not in such a state of, well,
let's call it what it was –
Horny to an incapacitating degree.

Have you ever been so thunder-struck smitten that you had no
choice but to freeze like a statue, with the fear that if you contract
even one single muscle anywhere in your body it could trigger a
humiliatingly unstoppable nuclear-meltdown public orgasm?

If you have, then you know exactly what I'm talking about.

And if you haven't, then the Fates have spared you.
Or forsaken you.

I suppose it depends on your perspective on the whole thing.

Consent

So important that you have to learn it viscerally
so you respect it enough to value what it really is...

Now you've crossed paths with The Trickster, by design!
Don't you know –
there's always a reason, a consent from the Higher Self,
for me to arrive in your story.
A call for discernment.

Therefore, as much as the Temporal Self writhes
at the sound of my Trickster's Bell,
which I regret to inform you cannot be unrung,
The Higher Self means this transformation to be so.

Just so.

Not everything that looks like hurt is harmful.
In the same way as what looks like help
certainly isn't always helpful.

Softer

In the Microcosm, the question to ask is:
Is this choice medicine or poison?

In the Macrocosm, the question to ask is:
Is this pattern medicine or poison?

Remember:
The goal is to become softer.

Drum Beats for Creation

Patient, Relentless, Resilient, Opportunistic.
Often you seem a total stranger to me,
And yet –

When I see a sprig of green poke through a crack in the sidewalk
A weed, any weed
The spires of my aloe leaning east
Or ivy crawling up the crumbling sides of an abandoned house
In some unincorporated dilapidated memory

Suddenly that pulsing force does not seem so foreign.
It rumbles in my chest.

It sings:

Give us a thousand bad days
Dam the rivers,
burn the trees,
Pave the earth,
And still.
All we need
is one moment of sunlight
and a few molecules of carbon
To make the best of it.

I close my eyes and acknowledge the seeds within me–
They are mine, and they will thrive in their own time.
The rhythm is encoded.

And the waiting for it is holy.

The Sermon of the Snowy Thursday Night

Okay big realization – I'm pretty sure for my whole life I have been confusing the concept of "the mission" with the concept of ACHIEVEMENT.

What do I mean by mission? In summary, I believe that each of us chose to come here, to incarnate on this planet, in order to learn something specific and particular to our soul family lineage, something that either neutralizes a harmful pattern we're carrying in our cosmic DNA and/or proliferates some helpful and divinely inspired gift that we're meant to bestow upon the world because the ultimate expansion of this universe is fueled by net-new experiences of bliss.

So you see, the mission can never be fully realized only by doing something. The mission is shaped, fundamentally, by *experiences* that impart *lessons*.

To be sure, this kind of learning still implies taking action. BUT not necessarily (and certainly not exclusively) the kind of action that I've been programmed to associate with achievement, aka to demonstrate an unmatched excellence in a thing, ideally in a way that secures positive external validation of said excellence, my excellence, my worthiness, my personhood... oh, and of course, the more of this kind of validation, the better!

I've been assuming this whole time that actions toward excellence are the only kinds of actions that are meaningful in the long run, that "count," when the reality is that the necessary actions I need to take to fully and completely learn the lessons that clear my karma and unlock my gifts (aka THE mission I came here for), these lessons are just as likely to come in the form of very humble and very private moments... through the subtle actions of conscious receiving, like:

- *How to ask for help*
- *How to listen to my own intuition*
- *How to sense the nuance between conditional and unconditional love*
- *How to be nourished*
- *How to be held*

What if I'm here simply to learn how to worship, anoint, and exfoliate my own two lips such that they are sanctified and ready to receive the world's most sublime first kiss?

What if I'm here to offer the most sincere "thank you" to every bus driver, grocery store clerk, and bank teller I come across, or master the art of laughing with my entire body in a way that subconsciously encourages everyone I meet to tell more jokes?

What if I came here to learn how to build a safe and loving home for a retired greyhound with bad hips, or hone a sixth sense for the exact moment to call an old friend out of the blue just to check in, or compulsively accumulate the perfect Poppins Bag so that someday I'm the lady on the airplane who just happens to have a band-aid and some stickers and a lollipop in my purse for the stressed out mom with the crying child with the nasty papercut booboo on her pinky finger who hasn't even been born yet??

What if I came here to learn one lesson, and one lesson only- how to relax, and breathe, and slow down time so much so that I become present enough to ecstatically witness one single crystalline snowflake land on the tip of my nose?

And then, voila!
The Gates of Nirvana are flung open before me!
Meanwhile, achievement via some external comparison-based measurement of excellence may have absolutely nothing to do with it!

Ironically (and tragically, I might add)... striving for achievement may be the exact thing that's been distracting me from receiving and sharing and noticing and connecting and aligning with the very lessons I actually came here to learn! In other words, fixating (and remember, where our attention goes, our energy flows) fixating ON achievement could be the very thing holding me back from achieving my mission!

< Pause to Scream into a Pillow >

The Alchemists teach us – fall in love with the process, fall in love the materials, and in doing so, excellence is inevitable.

I cannot say at this point that I've found that great all-consuming love yet, the kind of love that yields excellence as a casual byproduct... But I can't wait to learn what else the Alchemists have

to say about experiential, interpersonal, and service-based lessons, and how to consciously receive and allow. In fact, I might even feel the first fluttering stirs of a crush on this very idea, on this kind of learning, and so perhaps the doing that follows
might even be
quietly excellent
in its unfolding.

The Telepathy Tapes,
But Make It About Me

In a future paradigm where we are all psychic
And we can all communicate with one another telepathically,
Our thoughts will no longer be private.

And in order for us to be safe, and functional,
In community with one another
We will all be faced with this choice:

Whether to shine a sweeping bright beam into our own minds, And
not look away, but embrace all our scuttling infestations,
All those secrets, deepest shames, insecurities, and hypocrisies –

The ones that scatter reflexively
Like roaches under the light?

Or else...
Whether to cease thinking altogether.

Prophecy

Visions with no context sound like nonsense to the mind,
But feel, to the body, like prophecy.

The Way Home

My favorite thing on tv right now is a drama called *The Way Home*.

It's about three generations of women who live on a farm in New Brunswick, and on the property of the farm there's a magical pond that allows them to travel back in time, visiting key events in their family history that happened in the 1990's, the 1970's, 1814, and so on.

The only thing that frustrates me about this show is that these women, these characters, they only spend a small fraction of each episode actually time traveling.
They only jump in the pond and visit the past when they need to, in order to reconcile what's happening in their lives in the present.

If I lived in that world, in that fictional universe?
I'd be jumping in that pond *constantly*.
I wouldn't need a reason, beyond the thrill and the wonder.
I would become obsessed with the magic.
I would show no restraint. I would call it ascension.
And I would love every second of it.
But there's a shadow there.

I would lose all interest in the "mundanities" of the present. I'd become so enthralled with the past that I would stop creating my future. I would become addicted to the traveling, lost in time, and my own branch of the family tree would essentially self-prune.

I want so badly to experience magic, but I think, even more than that, I want to believe in something PURE.

Something that is all upside, all *good*, and the only shadow it could possibly cast would be its eventual loss.

But that is not the way of us children of the sun.
There is no posture on earth that doesn't cast a shadow.

Addiction, even to the "purity" of ascension,
is still a serpent devouring its own tail.
All teeth and tongue and hunger, with no sustainability.
All heart with no mercy.

The antidote to Addiction is Temperance,
but temperance doesn't mean Abstinence,
nor is it as simple as some "50/50" split for the sake of Balance.
It's learning how to weave the magic and the mundane together,
In deliberate shifting ratios of color and texture,
with deep skill and reverence for both,
each serving their part to transmute parts into something whole.
And this might even be a *process* of purification,
if we can weave the threads just so,
that every inevitable shadow is relationally balanced,
all blind spots and biases tempered by a Collective Light.

The Alchemists may urge us to fall in love with the process,
but the Zen Masters warn us:
Do not confuse the finger pointing at the moon
for the moon itself.

Do not confuse the teacher with the lesson.
I confess, I didn't really get that until just now.

And while I am devoted to ascension, and often quite enamored
with its magic and wonder,
I must learn to weave it into life with greater Temperance,
and appreciate it as just one part of the whole.
Ascension itself isn't wholeness.
Just as the pond itself is not home.
It is *the way* home.
The magic is just another thread, another part,
Another finger pointing at the moon.

Annihilated

By gods, I loved watching that man eat.

He was built lean and densely muscled, one of those natural athletes who'd been jogging for fun since he was a kid and still had the metabolism to match. Rode his bike a lot, like A LOT a lot, and definitely had the ass to match.

He was always hungry, but fairly particular when it came to food. Not picky per se, very adventurous, but he held his personal tastes strongly and, after growing up in the culinary bastion of Portland, he was accustomed to both skill and quality in a kitchen.

Now, keep all that in mind, and also know –
that he would still absolutely *annihilate* every meal I set down in front of him as if he'd just been pulled in from a shipwreck.

No utensils half the time, just pawing in with his bare hands and no shame. He might hesitate for a second if the spread was particularly good, waggling his fingers together like a cartoon villain.

And then the feral instinct would take over.

I once spent days assembling the *perfect* meatball sub, crafting each element from scratch. He devoured it in three bites, so fast he was actually panting afterwards to catch his breath and grinning glassy-eyed with marinara from ear to ear like a cannibal on ecstasy.

I swear I'm turning myself on right now just thinking about it.

I started devising menu plans that quite literally got saucier and saucier. Chutneys and gravies and runny yolks and salted butterscotch. Lacquered meats falling off the bone, with bread for dipping and sopping up juices. Baklava soaked in honeycomb, sticky dates wrapped in bacon with secret little pockets of oozing manchego.

He would have streaks of spicy curry running down his chin and in between his fingers, and I'd lose myself watching him trace his tongue down the side of his forearm to catch a rogue dribble and then suck the last bit of tikka from the end of his thumb.

Mm.
That's it.
That right there.
That's the memory.

The Beautiful Way

Remember these alchemizing phrases:

I bless this hurt.
I acknowledge it.
I open myself up to receive it,
and all the wisdom that it brings.
I bless this hurt with gratitude and compassion.
I bless this conscious allowing,
this path toward trust.
This Beautiful Way.

Toad Lady

Lay me down in the damp brush under a shady spot
And cover my body in toads
I want to feel their soft bumpy skin against my skin
I want to feel their tender bellies expand and contract
Digesting bits of cricket and mosquito
I want to feel the low croak of their toad-song
Like the doors of haunted houses
I want to see my reflection in the amphibian glass
Of their bulbous green-gold eyes
I want to learn how to breathe through my skin
And fold my own limbs up
So I can squat in coiled potential
Fat and happy
Under the shade
Like those tiny mighty Lords of Bog.
Those horny Princes of Mud.

Epilogue:
Don Quixote's Inner Monologue

Now I invite Nihilism in, to sit with me for tea.
Hello, My Darkness!
My old friend. I've come to talk with you again.

And my ego spasms between the white-knuckle dread that
everything is about to change
and the unbearable alternative –
that maybe nothing will change at all.
And maybe this world just is what it is,
and maybe I – just don't have the will to thrive in it.

AM I ascending right now, or am I just disintegrating?
Am I channeling Spirit through my words and deeds,
or manically scribbling at 3 am?
Am I the sovereign salvation of my own reality,
or the architect of my own mediocrity?
Am I reading the signs and portents correctly,
or am I losing my ever-loving mind?

Maybe Neither?
Maybe Both?
And either way – IS IT WORTH IT?

And aaaahhh. There She is, The Mystery,
The pulsing arterial vein of the matter.
The impossible question to answer
when you can feel into futures that you can't quite see yet.

Is it worth it?

The Open Query we demand of The Present.

Just how I imagine The Past surely wonders, "Are we doing ANY of
this right?" and The Future cries, "How the fuck did we get HERE?"
with equally desperate confusion.

The Mystery. The unanswerable questions. The almighty Always
Unknowable to each singular perspective at each singular point in
time.

And I gotta ask myself – can I live in this world of not knowing
without losing myself in The Mystery, without turning Her into
either my enemy or My Quest?

And fuck me, My Darkness laughs, *does it take a Holy Crusade just to
keep the existential dread at bay? Is that where we're at?*

Is that what all Saints have in common?
Nobody asked us to suffer. We choose it.

Why?

What is so hard to face on the other side of forsaken faith,
that martyrdom is the more attractive option?

Or is that you, Nihilism, distorting my view again...
Through a different facet of this same prism, couldn't we just as well
explore what heights of love and connection could inspire an
unwavering commitment?

Is it Neither?
Is it Both?

And the question remains...

IS IT WORTH IT?

And if the answer is yes – then great! Case closed!

Or maybe, well, now let's spend a moment on the question of
"What is enough?"
Because surely "what is enough" must define what is "worth it"
in the end, no?

And Oh, Christ! My Darkness, that'll take more than a moment, but
I think I can sum it up (unfortunately) with another question yet:
Is "Never Enough" the Great Sickness of our time, and thus mine?

Oooo-weee! Some questions are ephemeral.
This question is HEAVY.

Because what are the implications?

That I'm half-right, that I understood the role of fractals, just not the whole, and would that mean... that Capitalism – or at least the theory of free markets – is just another version of *my* Impossible Dream?

And better yet (or maybe worse),
wouldn't that then mean that the key to fulfillment
is actually pretty straightforward in this paradigm!?

Choosing to stop, to find contentment in exactly who one is, what one knows, what one has, to know abundance through gratitude alone is the clear answer – and then I immediately want to laugh and barf and faint with joyful horror, because this is an obvious and widely espoused truth that I've potentially been *wildly* underestimating for forty years, but –

Wait,
And don't get me wrong, I love gratitude, and part of me *does wish* it could all be that simple...
But something about that conclusion feels *too conclusive*.
Unsatisfying. *Itchy.*

Maybe the problem is that answering the unanswerable questions will rob The Mystery of Her power...
and that, that kills the soul just a little bit?
And I won't look at that, no, I don't want to see Her
with Her majestic head bowed low.

Or perhaps underneath all my rusted idealism,
my actual deal-breaker is not nearly so precious.

I won't look because once I see Her, powerful or not,
there will be no more need for my seeking.

So wait, am I to understand then that I'm not just afraid that it's
NOT worth it... I'm also afraid that it IS?? Because in either case,
the Animus of "Never Enough" is what's at stake?

And She, not The Mystery but The PURSUIT of Her, *She* is my true
Dulcinea, my sweet Dopamina, my agony and my ecstasy...

And what does it say about me, if The Pursuit is my reason?
Is there any nobility to be found in this process?
Can The Pursuit ever love me back?
How can I feel so lost, when this coffee mug I'm holding assures me
that the journey is more important than the destination...

Am I asking too much of The Mystery
because chivalry *needs* to be needed?
What differentiates a reason from an excuse?
Am I fighting giants in Her name because even a windmill is more
interesting than waking up again and again just to grind out another
Monday?

IF there is any *real love* in all this valor, wouldn't the noblest act of
middle age be to once and for all – let The Mystery go?
And turn my gaze down to the ground I actually stand on, and set
my hands to work in a more immediate service?

Neither? Both?

And My Darkness whispers: *That's an awfully big IF…*

And underneath that, the lens keeps widening, widening,
until I am standing eye to eye with –

All or Nothing.
Have I expanded so much that, paradoxically,
my ultimate choice is binary?
Could "All or Nothing" turn out to be the Highest Truth,
if I could just parse the data correctly?
Could I access every earthly delight,
so long as I accept the suffering that comes along with it?
Is this *the only* truth left for me,
now that I've tried and failed to withstand The Nothing?
Now that I've seen how denying delight just breeds other forms of
suffering?

And isn't this the exact "Devil's Bargain" that I've been taught to
fear my whole Catholic life?

And speaking of Catholics, wouldn't it make sense to vilify
both The All and The Nothing,
if our Oppressors aim to keep us stuck in the middle?

And speaking of our Oppressors, it is *so hard* to answer these
questions when all I can hear inside my head is – "WHO is the

SUCKER in this equation? Which one of us is the fool? The one who believes All? Or the one who believes Nothing?"

Neither of us?
Both?

Why are we so intent on finding fault, I ask My Darkness,
as I pour Him another cup.
Why force this polarity on me?
Why does someone else have to be wrong
in order for me to be right?
Isn't THAT the ultimate scam, and we are ALL the suckers
because we are The Sleeping Gods
who keep hitting the snooze button?

There's only one way to find out.

So with no small amount of panic, I take a deep breath,
I consent.

I tell My Darkness – Fine! Yes! If it really is All or Nothing, then I say gimme it All, for better and for worse, and not because I'm afraid of The Nothing this time, but because I sense that The All contains *such beauty*, and I can't accept anything less. And then I immediately want to laugh and barf and faint with joyful horror, I want to un-consent and give it back, not because the road to All ends abruptly in Hell –

But because staring right into the face of Source-God will bleach the bones of those who attempt it, one way or another.

Because the opposite of an extreme is still an extreme.

And I see All and see that it is what it is.
And All contains beauty, and hope, and love,
And My Beloved Darkness, He never leaves my table.
And I learn how to make a home for Him inside my own mind,
which never stops expanding into I am, That I am.

And it turns out *this just is* what it is,
To feel into futures that you can't quite see yet:

It is equal parts Madness and Grace.